A LIFE THROUGH FLOWERS

BY C B. MAY

For the Gardeners in my life.
Thank you for teaching me to see,
and not just look.

Contents

I   Introduction

II   Daisy Chain, an Ode to

III   Freshly Fallen

IV   Dear Cactus

V   My Tulips

VI   My Love, My Life, My Lilly

VII   Finding my Green Thumb

INTRODUCTION

I come from a matriarchal line of 'Green Thumbs', yet it seemed mine were obtusely brown. I brought decay to greenery of all lines of care, purchased for decorations. I even managed to singe the threaded fabrics of fake florals. That 'pop of colour' very soon became a stink no amount of airing could release. Orchids suffered upon my brutalist windowsill, flowing in the dry air of a young girls room before they wilted away to the healing arms of my mother. Stunning scents faded in the never-opening curtains as I shrivelled more with each empty pot.

I could not have possibly done anything wrong. I considered myself the master of their care. I bought all the supplements (and used them generously), watered them when I remembered (which I must admit I did not), and treasured each pot of life brought forth to me. I was too young to understand the roots fleeing the pot needed my attention, or that the harsh rays of the summer sun through my window could scorch their delicate petals. The only possible explanation to me? The Green Thumb must have skipped a generation, bounced right off of my gene pool. I just wasn't cut out for it, I was in store for a life stripped of all plants. Potted or otherwise, I was done. Not to mention the curse of hay fever that forced me into hiding throughout spring. 'Wake up and smell the roses', and sneeze as soon as you do.

I decided there was nothing to do but accept that I was forever cursed to live in envy of the ritualistic route of my Nanny in the mornings. Tea in one hand, watering can in the other, gently relieving her hoard of herbs from their thirst and hunting the hydrangeas in need of her helping hand. Even now I go to find her in her conservatory giving the army of home-grown bonsais a well needed trim and wire them into perfection. Of course my Grandad would call her a 'Crazy Plant Lady', but everyone knew better than to ask him about his model trains. I love to watch as he rolls his eyes watching Nanny load a trolley with bulbs for next season, yet always points out the perfect pot for her latest plant passion project. Behind every huff and puff, he loves her more than life, and she may even love him more than plants.

What was my inspiration for this collection? The dedication my family has put into the finite details of every bit of flora around them. To pay attention to the finest details of their care, country of origin, even their Latin names. To love something so deeply that the details just stuck in your mind like glue. Plants have been such a large part of my life, whether voluntary or not. And what better way to tell the story of my life than by diving into the world of floriography.

I may not have been born with a green thumb, but I am determined to love plants as they do. Even if it means painting my thumb green.

DAISY CHAIN, AN ODE TO GIRLHOOD

Bellis perennis

For innocence, loyalty, and an ability to keep things secret.

I will tie us to my memories
Link each with gentle hands
Piercing a hole in the stem
With soft, unshaped nails
Sat in a circle amongst girls
Just names in the photo album now

We grew into beautiful women
And now I weave you into
An ode to my girlhood
Spent in the mud with you
Linking the chains together
To place a crown upon our heads

The daisies grow now
As spring peels open the sun
Opening at the break of the morning

To be picked by girls new,

Girls yet to grow up

Girls with nothing in common,

But grazes on their knees

And crowns of daisies upon

Their wonderful, growing, minds.

FRESHLY FALLEN

Autumnus

Originally written together with my Nanny, walking is art.

It was a cold bright morning,
    Novembers deepest day.
        We walked towards the lake
            Hand in hand
                The leaves from mighty giants
                Fell down around us
                    The world stilled for a moment
                For time was too young for me
            Caught in the sight of decay
            Picturesque in shades of crimson
        Twas lovely to behold,
    Mothers wonder surrounded us

Beneath the great oak, acorns fell
    Hats for mighty warriors
        Conjured from the childish mind
            To fight in a war against Jack Frost
                As it bit and snatched at delving roots
                    Hand in loving hand we watched

    The whispers
        of life
            ending
                Engulfed
                    with the life
                      to follow

DEAR CACTUS

Cactaceae

For strength, endurance, and protection.

Dear cactus, scrambling for the sun

On the windowsill of a girl too young

Sat in a pot, a lonely king

Waiting for the single bloom summer will bring

The halo of spines circle its form

A rose could not compare to these thorns

A rare and isolated sight to see

A desert treasure, kept from being free

A survivor of my ruthless hand

The trials of time it will withstand

The thirst unwilling to subside

Yet wilt you not from your time inside

Dear cactus, you do endure me

Thriving in this depravity

I even sit and see you grow

In this castle upon which you were thrown

MY TULIPS

Tulipa

*For perfect or deep love, rebirth...or **charity***

To gift a bouquet means to

Use your love, know her heart, and

Look for that which she treasures.

Indubitably declare to her;

My Darling, I Love you!

Yet my Tulipa...

Please, *hold me in your arms as if it were yesterday.*

So *tenderly, Love me once again.*

MY LOVE, MY LIFE, MY LILY

Lilium

For sweetness, purity, femininity, love.

    With each blink of an eye you bloom
My love, my life, my Lily
    My tongue ties at your smile
My love, my life, my Lily
    Poetry falls short of your laugh
My love, my life, my Lily
    Your heart has room for the world
My love, my life, my Lily
    And you open it up for mine
My love, my life, my Lily
    If I could say all this to you
My love, my life, my Lily
    I would be more than a poet
My love, my life, my Lily

I am yours, my heart beats only for you

Forever, from now, until I lay with the earth

I am yours

My heart, my soul,

My love, my life, my Lily

FINDING MY GREEN THUMB

Monstera deliciosa Liebm aka. The Cheese Plant

For grandiose plans, glad tidings, and deep relationships.

Maybe, a green thumb isn't something you were born with. Maybe a green thumb is about finding what you love, a little monstera sprout wasting away on a sale section. It's about bringing that little sprout home, freeing it from the suffocating pot. Gently easing the dirt off of the roots, untangling them while they gasp for more space. It's about digging a bigger pot out of the gardening box and positioning myself amongst the grass, bag of dirt in my lap. Gently spooning a blanket of dirt upon the bottom of the pot, preventing the roots from falling from their gentle throne. Easing the dirt up the sides of the pot before lowering the sprout into its new haven. Once it settles into the rich dirt surrounding it, lowering it into a gentle bath of water. Allowing it to soak up only as much as it needs. No longer drowning them because I care too much, or letting them wilt and fade away for caring too little. And watching as that sprout grows, new leaves bursting from stems in curled up spears. Detangling them from the holes of the cheese plant, ensuring they have room to relax. One day, through this gentle care, that sprout will be a king. Producing sprouts of its own, held up by supports I lovingly installed to stop it from faltering. That sprout is now perfectly positioned beside me as I write, looking over my work.

My green thumb isn't nurturing bonsais like my Nanny's is, it isn't spending early spring winding branches into place while their bark is soft and malleable. Or trimming away the branches that don't make sense in the composition. So brutal, yet beautiful. It isn't my mother's love for Orchids, placing them upon each windowsill of the house. Filling the bathroom with their vibrance, misting them when they need her healing hand. Or my stepmothers blooming bush-plants. Filling bowls instead of pots, gifting their sprouts to the family. Holding her breath while she repots them in the summer, a passionate carer.

Looking at where I had been, at the women surrounding me, it was easy to feel as if I fell short. As if I wasn't the florist they were, and therefore could never be. I put so much pressure on myself to be just as they are, to become them. But the fact is, you don't become the people before you. You are inspired by them, shaped by them, yes. But you have always been your own. I had found my green thumb buried in the plants needing care. The plants overlooked and underappreciated. Now, I sit amongst my plants, big leaved and large stemmed. My room filled to the brim with them, each surface littered with life. Realising that I have a green thumb after all, it does run in the family. Not in the way I thought it was, not wired into the very fabric of my genetics. But rather in the way I was brought up, nurtured as gently and lovingly as the plants surrounding me. By wonderful women, mothers, friends. I could not have asked for a better family, or a more green thumb. Through my Life of Flowers, I found why I love them so. Nature brings so many together, has such bountiful history. It would be impossible not to love flora of any kind, or to find the language of flowers in everything you've done.

Perhaps this sounds like the plea of a newfound crazy plant lady, but when something wonderful happens, look for a flower. Whether it be a Daisy for your childhood, a Tulip for your heartbreaks, or a Lily for the love of

your life. Flowers are everything,
everyone, every moment.

Printed in Great Britain
by Amazon